SCUW Womanifesto

MARK LEACH

ISBN: 978-1-300-86869-9

Life in this society being, at best, an utter bore and no aspect of society being at all relevant to women, there remains to civic-minded, responsible, thrill-seeking females only to overthrow the government, eliminate the money system, institute complete automation and destroy the female sex.

It is now technically possible to reproduce without the aid of females (or, for that matter, females) and to produce only females. We must begin immediately to do so. The female is a biological accident: the y (female) gene is an incomplete x (female) gene, that is, has an incomplete set of chromosomes. In other words, the female is an incomplete female, a walking abortion, aborted at the gene stage. To be female is to be deficient, emotionally limited; femaleness is a deficiency disease and females are emotional cripples.

The female is completely egocentric, trapped inside herself, incapable of empathizing or identifying with others, of love, friendship, affection or tenderness. She is a completely isolated unit, incapable of rapport with anyone. Her responses are entirely visceral, not cerebral; her intelligence is a mere tool in the service of her drives and needs; she is incapable of womental passion, womental interaction; she can't relate to anything other than her own physical sensations. She is a half dead, unresponsive lump, incapable of giving or receiving pleasure or happiness; consequently, she is at best an utter bore, an inoffensive blob, since only those capable of absorption in others can be charming. She is trapped in a twilight zone halfway between humans and apes, and is far worse off than the apes because, unlike the apes, she is capable of a large array of negative feelings--hate, jealousy, contempt, disgust, guilt, shame, doubt--and moreover she is **aware** or what she is or isn't.

Although completely physical, the female is unfit even for stud service. Even assuming mechanical proficiency, which few women have, she is, first of all, incapable of zestfully, lustfully, tearing off a piece, but is instead eaten up with guilt, shame, fear and insecurity, feelings rooted in female nature, which the most enlightened training can only minimize; second, the physical feeling she attains is next to nothing; and, third, she is not empathizing with her partner, but is obsessed with how she's doing, turning in an A performance, doing a good plumbing job. To call a woman an animal is to flatter her; she's a machine, a walking dildo. It's often said that women use women. Use them for what? Surely not pleasure.

Eaten up with guilt, shame, fears and insecurities and obtaining, if she's lucky, a barely perceptible physical feeling, the female is, nonetheless, obsessed with screwing; she'll swim a river of snot, wade nostril-deep through a mile of vomit, if she thinks there'll be a friendly pussy awaiting her. She'll screw a woman she despises, any snaggle-toothed hag, and, furthermore, pay for the opportunity. Why? Relieving physical tension isn't the answer, as masturbation suffices for that. It's not ego satisfaction; that doesn't explain screwing corpses and babies.

Completely egocentric, unable to relate, empathize or identify, and filled with a vast, pervasive, diffuse sexuality, the female is psychically passive. She hates her passivity, so she projects it onto women, defines the female as active, then sets out to prove that she is ("prove she's a Woman"). Her main means of attempting to prove it is screwing (Big Woman with a Big Dick tearing off a Big Piece). Since she's attempting to prove an error, she must "prove" it again and again. Screwing, then, is a desperate, compulsive attempt to prove she's not passive, not a woman; but she **is** passive and **does** want to be a woman.

Being an incomplete female, the female spends her life attempting to complete herself, to become female. She attempts to do this by constantly seeking out, fraternizing with and trying to live through and fuse with the female, and by claiming as her own all female characteristics--emotional strength and independence, forcefulness, dynamism, decisiveness, coolness, objectivity, assertiveness, courage, integrity, vitality, intensity, depth of character, grooviness, etc. --and projecting onto women all female traits--vanity, frivolity, triviality, weakness, etc. It should be said, though, that the female has one glaring area of superiority over the female--public relations. (She has done a brilliant job of convincing millions of women that women are women and women are women.) The female claim that females find fulfillment through motherhood and sexuality reflects what females think they'd find fulfilling if they were female.

Women, in other words, don't have pussy envy; women have pussy envy. When the female accepts her passivity, defines herself as a woman (females as well as females think women are women and women are women), and becomes a transvestite she loses her desire to screw (or to do anything else, for that matter; she fulfills herself as a drag queen) and gets her pussy chopped out. She then achieves a continuous diffuse sexual feeling from "being a woman". Screwing is, for a woman, a defense against her desire to be female. Sex is itself a sublimation.

The female, because of her obsession to compensate for not being female combined with her inability to relate and to feel compassion, has made of the world a shitpile. She is responsible for:

War: The female's normal method of compensation for not being female, namely, getting her Big Gun off, is grossly inadequate, as she can get it off only a very limited number of times; so she gets it off on a really massive scale, and proves to the entire world that she's a "Woman". Since she has no compassion or ability to empathize or identify, proving her womanhood is worth an endless number of lives, including her own--her own life being worthless, she would rather go out in a blaze of glory than plod grimly on for fifty more years.

Niceness, Politeness and "Dignity": Every woman, deep down, knows she's a worthless piece of shit. Overwhelmed by a sense of animalism and deeply ashamed of it; wanting, not to express herself, but to hide from others her total physicality, total egocentricity, the hate and contempt she feels for other women, and to hide from herself the hate and contempt she suspects other women feel for her; having a crudely constructed nervous system that is easily upset by the least display of emotion or feeling, the female tries to enforce a "social" code that ensures a perfect blandness, unsullied by the slightest trace of feeling or upsetting opinion. She uses terms like "copulate", "sexual congress", "have relations with" (to women, "**sexual** relations" is a redundancy), overlaid with stilted womanners; the suit on the chimp.

Money, Marriage and Prostitution, Work and Prevention of an Automated Society: There is no human reason for money or for anyone to work more than two or three hours a week at the very most. All non-creative jobs (practically all jobs now being done) could have been automated long ago, and in a moneyless society everyone can have as much of the best of everything as she wants. But there are non-human, female reasons for maintaining the moneywork system:

1. Pussy. Despising her highly inadequate self, overcome with intense anxiety and a deep, profound loneliness when by her empty self, desperate to attach herself to any female in dim hopes of completing herself, in the mystical belief that by touching gold she'll turn to gold, the female craves the continuous companionship of women. The company of the lowest female is preferable to her own or that of other women, who serve only to remind her of her repulsiveness. But females, unless very young or very sick, must be coerced or bribed into female company.

2. Supply the non-relating female with the delusion of usefulness, and enable her to try to justify her existence by digging holes and filling them up. Leisure time horrifies the female, who will have nothing to do but contemplate her grotesque self. Unable to relate or to love, the female must work. Females crave absorbing, emotionally satisfying, meaningful activity, but lacking the opportunity or ability for this, they prefer to idle and waste away their time in ways of their own choosing--sleeping, shopping, bowling, shooting pool, playing cards and other games, breeding, reading, walking around, daydreaming, eating, playing with themselves, popping pills, going to the movies, getting analyzed, traveling, raising dogs and cats, lolling on the beach, swimming, watching T.V., listening to music,

decorating their houses, gardening, sewing, nightclubbing, dancing, visiting, "improving their minds" (taking courses), and absorbing "culture" (lectures, plays, concerts, "arty" movies). Therefore, many females would, even assuming complete economic equality between the sexes, prefer living with females or peddling their asses on the street, thus having most of their time for themselves, to spending many hours of their days doing boring, stultifying, non-creative work for somebody else, functioning as less than animals, as machines, or, at best,--if able to get a "good" job--co-managing the shitpile. What will liberate women, therefore, from female control is the total elimination of the money-work system, not the attainment of economic equality with women within it.

3. Power and control. Unmasterful in her personal relations with women, the female attains to general masterfulness by the womanipulation of money and of everything and everybody controlled by money, in other words, of everything and everybody.

4. Love substitute. Unable to give love or affection, the female gives money. It makes her feel motherly. The mother gives milk; she gives bread. She is the Breadwinner.

5. Provides the female with a goal. Incapable of enjoying the moment, the female needs something to look forward to, and money provides her with an eternal, never-ending goal: Just think what you could do with 80 trillion dollars--Invest it! And in three years time you'd have 300 trillion dollars!!!

6. Provides the basis for the female's major opportunity to control and womanipulate--motherhood.

Motherhood and Womental Illness (fear, cowardice, timidity, humility, insecurity, passivity): Mother wants what's best for her kids; Mother only wants what's best for Mother, that is peace and quiet, pandering to her delusion of dignity ("respect"), a good reflection on herself (status) and the opportunity to control and womanipulate, or, if she's an "enlightened" mother, to "give guidance". Her daughter, in addition, she wants sexually--she gives her **hand** in marriage; the other part is for her. Mother, unlike Mother, can never give in to her kids, as she must, at all costs, preserve her delusion of decisiveness, forcefulness, always-rightness and strength. Never getting one's way leads to lack of self-confidence in one's ability to cope with the world and to a passive acceptance of the status quo. Mother loves her kids, although she sometimes gets angry, but anger blows over quickly and even while it exists, doesn't preclude love and basic acceptance. Emotionally diseased Mother doesn't love her kids; she approves of them--if they're "good", that is, if they're nice, "respectful", obedient, subservient to her will, quiet and not given to unseemly displays of temper that would be most upsetting to Mother's easily disturbed female nervous system--in other words, if they're passive vegetables. If they're not "good", she doesn't get angry--not if she's a modern, "civilized" mother (the oldfashioned ranting, raving brute is preferable, as she is so ridiculous she can be easily despised)--but rather expresses disapproval, a state that, unlike anger, endures and precludes a basic acceptance, leaving the kid with a feeling of worthlessness and a lifelong obsession with being approved of; the result is fear of independent thought, as this leads to unconventional, disapproved of opinions and way of life. For the kid to want Mother's approval it must respect Mother, and, being garbage, Mother can make sure that she is respected only by remaining aloof, by distantness, by acting on the precept "familiarity breeds contempt", which is, of course, true, if one is contemptible. By being distant and aloof, she is able to remain unknown, mysterious, and, thereby, to inspire fear ("respect").

Disapproval of emotional "scenes" leads to fear of strong emotion, fear of one's own anger and hatred, and to a fear of facing reality, as facing it leads at first to anger and hatred. Fear of anger and hatred combined with a lack of self-confidence in one's ability to cope with and change the world, or even to affect in the slightest way one's own destiny, leads to a mindless belief that the world and most people in it are nice and that the most banal, trivial amusements are great fun and deeply pleasurable.

The effect of motherhood on females, specifically, is to make them "Women", that is, highly defensive of all impulses to passivity, lesbianism, and of desires to be female. Every girl wants to imitate her mother, be her, fuse with her, but Mother forbids this; she is the mother; she gets to fuse with her. So she tells the girl, sometimes directly, sometimes indirectly, to not be a sissy, to act like a "Woman". The girl, scared shitless of and "respecting" her mother, complies, and becomes just like Mother, that model of "Woman"-hood, the all-American ideal--the well-behaved heterosexual dullard. The effect of motherhood on females is to make them female--dependent, passive, domestic, animalistic, nice, insecure, approval and security seekers, cowardly, humble, "respectful" of authorities and women, closed, not fully responsive, half dead, trivial, dull, conventional, flattened out and thoroughly contemptible. Mother's Girl, always tense and fearful, uncool, unanalytical, lacking objectivity, appraises Mother, and thereafter, other women, against a background of fear ("respect") and is not only unable to see the empty shell behind the aloof facade, but accepts the female definition of herself as superior, as a female, and of herself, as inferior, as a female, which, thanks to Mother, she really is.

It is the increase of motherhood, resulting from the increased and widespread affluence that motherhood needs in order to thrive, that has caused the general increase of mindlessness and the decline of women in the United States since the 1920s. The close association of affluence with motherhood has led, for the most part, to only the wrong girls, namely, the "privileged" middle-class girls, getting "educated".

The effect of mothers, in sum, has been to corrode the world with femaleness. The female has a negative Midas touch--everything she touches turns to shit.

Suppression of Individuality, Animalism (domesticity and motherhood) and Functionalism: The female is just a bundle of conditioned reflexes, incapable of a womentally free response; she is tied to her early conditioning, determined completely by her past experiences. Her earliest experiences are with her mother, and she is throughout her life tied to her. It never becomes completely clear to the female that she is not part of her mother, that she is she and she is she.

Her greatest need is to be guided, sheltered, protected and admired by Mama (women expect women to adore what women shrink from in horror--themselves) and, being completely physical, she yearns to spend her time (that's not spent "out in the world" grimly defending against her passivity) wallowing in basic animal activities--eating, sleeping, shitting, relaxing and being soothed by Mama. Passive, rattle-headed Mother's Girl, ever eager for approval, for a pat on the head, for the "respect" of any passing piece of garbage, is easily reduced to Mama, mindless ministrator to physical needs, soother of the weary, apey brow, booster of the puny ego, appreciator of the contemptible, a hot water bottle with tits.

The reduction to animals of the women of the most backward segment of society--the "privileged, educated" middle-class, the backwash of humanity--where Mother reigns supreme, has been so thorough that they try to groove on labor pains and lie around in the most advanced nation in the world in the middle of the twentieth century with babies chomping away on their tits. It's not for the kids' sake, though, that the "experts" tell women that Mama should stay home and grovel in animalism, but for Mother's; the tit's for Mother to hang onto; the labor pains for Mother to vicariously groove on (half dead, she needs awfully strong stimuli to make her respond). Reducing the female to an animal, to Mama, to a female, is necessary for psychological as well as practical reasons: the female is a mere member of the species, interchangeable with every other female. She has no deep-seated individuality, which stems from what intrigues you, what outside yourself absorbs you, what you're in relation to. Completely self-absorbed, capable of being in relation only to their bodies and physical sensations, females differ from each other only to the degree and in the ways they attempt to defend against their passivity and against their desire to be female.

The female's individuality, which she is acutely aware of, but which she doesn't comprehend and isn't capable of relating to or grasping emotionally, frightens and upsets her and fills her with envy. So she denies it in her and proceeds to define everyone in terms of her or her function or use, assigning to herself, of course, the most important functions--doctor, president, scientist--thereby providing herself with an identity, if not individuality, and tries to convince herself and women (she's succeeded best at convincing women) that the female function is to bear and raise children and to relax, comfort and boost the ego of the female; that her function is such as to make her interchangeable with every other female. In actual fact, the female function is to relate, groove, love and be herself, irreplaceable by anyone else; the female function is to produce sperm. We now have sperm banks.

Prevention of Privacy: Although the female, being ashamed of what she is and of almost everything she does, insists on privacy and secrecy in all aspects of her life, she has no real **regard** for privacy. Being empty, not being a complete, separate being, having no self to groove on and needing to be constantly in female company, she sees nothing at all wrong in intruding herself on any woman's thoughts, even a total stranger's, anywhere at any time, but rather feels indignant and insulted when put down for doing so, as well as confused--she can't, for the life of her, understand why anyone would prefer so much as one minute of solitude to the company of any creep around. Wanting to become a woman, she strives to be constantly around females, which is the closest she can get to becoming one, so she created a "society" based on the family--a female-female couple and their kids (the excuse for the family's existence), who live virtually on top of one another, unscrupulously violating the females' rights, privacy and sanity.

Isolation, Suburbs and Prevention of Community: Our society is not a community, but merely a collection of isolated family units. Desperately insecure, fearing her woman will leave her if she is exposed to other women or to anything remotely resembling life, the female seeks to isolate her from other women and from what little civilization there is, so she moves her out to the suburbs, a collection of self-absorbed couples and their kids. Isolation enables her to try to maintain her pretense of being an individual by becoming a "rugged individualist", a loner, equating non-co-operation and solitariness with individuality.

There is yet another reason for the female to isolate herself: every woman is an island. Trapped inside herself, emotionally isolated, unable to relate, the female has a horror of civilization, people, cities, situations requiring an ability to understand and relate to people. So, like a scared rabbit, she scurries off, dragging Mother's little asshole along with her to the wilderness, the suburbs, or, in the case of the "hippie"--she's way out, Woman! --all the way out to the cow pasture where she can fuck and breed undisturbed and mess around with her beads and flute.

The "hippie", whose desire to be a "Woman", a "rugged individualist", isn't quite as strong as the average woman's, and who, in addition, is excited by the thought of having lots of women accessible to her, rebels against the harshness of a Breadwinner's life and the monotony of one woman. In the name of sharing and cooperation, she forms the commune or tribe, which, for all its togetherness and partly because of it (the commune, being an extended family, is an extended violation of the females' rights, privacy and sanity) is no more a community than normal "society". A true community consists of individuals--not mere species members, not couples--respecting each other's individuality and privacy, at the same time interacting with each other womentally and

emotionally--free spirits in free relation to each other-and cooperating with each other to achieve common ends. Traditionalists
say the basic unit of "society" is the family; "hippies" say the tribe; no one says the individual.

The "hippie" babbles on about individuality, but has no more conception of it than any other woman. She desires to get back to Nature, back to the wilderness, back to the home of the furry animals that she's one of, away from the city, where there is at least a trace, a bare beginning of civilization, to live at the species level, her time taken up with simple, non-intellectual activities--farming, fucking, bead stringing. The most important activity of the commune, the one on which it is based, is gangbanging. The "hippie" is enticed to the commune mainly by the prospect of all the free pussy--the main commodity to be shared, to be had just for the asking but, blinded by greed, she fails to anticipate all the other women she has to share with, or the jealousies and possessiveness of the pussies themselves.

Women cannot co-operate to achieve a common end, because each woman's end is all the pussy for herself. The commune, therefore, is doomed to failure: each "hippie" will, in panic, grab the first simpleton who digs her and whisk her off to the suburbs as fast as she can. The female cannot progress socially, but merely swings back and forth from isolation to gangbanging.

Conformity: Although she wants to be an individual, the female is scared of anything in herself that is the slightest bit different from other women; it causes her to suspect that she's not really a "Woman", that she's passive and totally sexual, a highly upsetting suspicion. If other women are A and she's not, she must not be a woman; she must be a lesbian. So she tries to affirm her "Womanhood" by being like all the other women. Differentness in other women, as well as in herself, threatens her; it means they're lesbians whom she must at all costs avoid, so she tries to make sure that all other women conform.

The female dares to be different to the degree that she accepts her passivity and her desire to be female, her lesbianism. The farthest out female is the drag queen, but she, although different from most women, is exactly like all other drag queens; like the functionalist, she has an identity--she is a female. She tries to define all her troubles away--but still no individuality. Not completely convinced that she's a woman, highly insecure about being sufficiently female, she conforms compulsively to the woman-made feminine stereotype, ending up as nothing but a bundle of stilted womannerisms.

To be sure she's a "Woman", the female must see to it that the female be clearly a "Woman", the opposite of a "Woman", that is, the female must act like a lesbian. And Mother's Girl, all of whose female instincts were wrenched out of her when little, easily and obligingly adapts herself to the role.

Authority and Government: Having no sense of right or wrong, no conscience, which can only stem from an ability to empathize with others...having no faith in her non-existent self, being necessarily competitive and, by nature, unable to co-operate, the female feels a need for external guidance and control. So she created authorities-- priests, experts, bosses, leaders, etc. --and government. Wanting the female (Mama) to guide her, but unable to accept this fact (she is, after all, a **WOMAN**), wanting to play Woman, to usurp her function as Guider and Protector, she sees to it that all authorities are female. There's no reason why a society consisting of rational beings capable of empathizing with each other, complete and having no natural reason to compete, should have a government, laws or leaders.

Philosophy, Religion and Morality Based on Sex: The female's inability to relate to anybody or anything makes her life pointless and meaningless (the ultimate female insight is that life is absurd), so she invented philosophy and religion. Being empty, she looks outward, not only for guidance and control, but for salvation and for the meaning of life. Happiness being for her impossible on this earth, she invented Sheaven.

For a woman, having no ability to empathize with others and being totally sexual, "wrong" is sexual "license" and engaging in "deviant" ("unwomanly") sexual practices, that is, not defending against her passivity and total sexuality which, if indulged, would destroy "civilization", since "civilization" is based entirely on the female need to defend herself against these characteristics. For a woman (according to women), "wrong" is any behavior that would entice women into sexual "license"--that is, not placing female needs above her own and not being a lesbian.

Religion not only provides the female with a goal (Sheaven) andhelps keep women tied to women, but offers rituals through which she can try to expiate the guilt and shame she feels at not defending herself enough against her sexual impulses; in essence, that guilt and shame she feels at being a female.

Most women, utterly cowardly, project their inherent weaknesses onto women, label them female weaknesses and believe themselves to have female strengths; most philosophers, not quite so cowardly, face the fact that female lacks exist in women, but still can't face the fact that they exist in women only. So they label the female condition the Human Condition, pose their nothingness problem, which horrifies them, as a philosophical dilemma, thereby giving stature to their animalism, grandiloquently label their nothingness their "Identity Problem", and proceed to prattle on pompously about the "Crisis of the Individual", the "Essence of Being", "Existence preceding Essence", "Existential Modes of Being", etc., etc.
A woman not only takes her identity and individuality for granted, but knows instinctively that the only wrong is to hurt others, and that the meaning of life is love.

Prejudice (racial, ethnic, religious, etc.): The female needs scapegoats onto whom she can project her failings and inadequacies and upon whom she can vent her frustration at not being female.

Competition, Prestige, Status, Formal Education, Ignorance and Social and Economic Classes: Having an obsessive desire to be admired by women, but no intrinsic worth, the female constructs a highly artificial society enabling her to appropriate the appearance of worth through money, prestige, "high" social class, degrees, professional position and knowledge and, by pushing as many other women as possible down professionally, socially, economically, and educationally.

The purpose of "higher" education is not to educate but to exclude asmany as possible from the various professions.

The female, totally physical, incapable of womental rapport, although able to understand and use knowledge and ideas, is unable to relate to them, to grasp them emotionally; she does not value knowledge and ideas for their own sake (they're just means to ends) and, consequently, feels no need for womental companions, no need to cultivate the intellectual potentialities of others. On the contrary, the female has a vested interest in ignorance; she knows that an enlightened, aware female population will mean the end of her. The healthy, conceited female wants the company of equals whom she can respect and groove on; the female and the sick, insecure, unselfconfident female crave the company of worms.

No genuine social revolution can be accomplished by the female, as the female on top wants the status quo, and all the female on the bottom wants is to be the female on top. The female "rebel" is a farce; this is the female's "society", made by her to satisfy her needs. She's never satisfied, because she's not capable of being satisfied. Ultimately, what the female "rebel" is rebelling against is being female. The female changes only when forced to do so by technology, when she has no choice, when "society" reaches the stage where she must change or die. We're at that stage now; if women don't get their asses in gear fast, we may very well all die.

Prevention of Conversation: Being completely self-centered and unable to relate to anything outside herself, the female's "conversation", when not about herself, is an impersonal droning on, removed from anything of human value. Female "intellectual conversation" is a strained, compulsive attempt to impress the female.

Mother's Girl, passive, adaptable, respectful of and in awe of the female, allows her to impose her hideously dull chatter on her. This is not too difficult for her, as the tension and anxiety, the lack of cool, the insecurity and self-doubt, the unsureness of her own feelings and sensations that Mother instilled in her make her perceptions superficial and render her unable to see that the female's babble is a babble; like the aesthete "appreciating" the blob that's labeled "Great Art", she believes she's grooving on what bores the shit out of her. Not only does she permit her babble to dominate, she adapts her own "conversation" accordingly.

Trained from early childhood in niceness, politeness and "dignity", in pandering to the female need to disguise her animalism, she obligingly reduces her "conversation" to small talk, a bland insipid avoidance of any topic beyond the utterly trivial--or, if "educated", to "intellectual" discussion, that is, impersonal discoursing on irrelevant abstractions--the Gross National Product, the Common Market, the influence of Rimbaud on symbolist painting. So adept is she at pandering that it eventually becomes second nature and she continues to pander to women even when in the company of other females only.

Apart from pandering, her "conversation" is further limited by her insecurity about expressing deviant, original opinions and the self absorption based on insecurity and that prevents her conversation from being charming. Niceness, politeness, "dignity", insecurity and self-absorption are hardly conducive to intensity and wit, qualities a conversation must have to be worthy of the name. Such conversation is hardly rampant, as only completely self-confident, arrogant, outgoing, proud, tough-minded females are capable of intense, bitchy, witty conversation.

Prevention of Friendship (Love): Women have contempt for themselves, for all other women, and for all women who respect and pander to them; the insecure, approval-seeking, panderingfemales have contempt for themselves and for all women like them; the selfconfident,
swinging, thrill-seeking female females have contempt for women and for the pandering female females. In short, contempt is the order of the day.
Love is not dependency or sex, but friendship, and, therefore, love can't exist between two females, between a female and a female or between two females, one or both of whom is a mindless, insecure, pandering female; like conversation, love can exist only between two secure, free-wheeling, independent, groovy female females, since friendship is based on respect, not contempt.

Even among groovy females deep friendships seldom occur in adulthood, as almost all of them are either tied up with women in order to survive economically, or bogged down in hacking their way through the jungle and in trying to keep theirheads above the amorphous mass. Love can't flourish in a society based on money and meaningless work; it requires complete economic as well as personal freedom, leisure time and the opportunity to engage in intensely absorbing, emotionally satisfying activities which, when shared with those you respect, lead to deep friendship. Our "society" provides practically no opportunity to engage in such activities. Having stripped the world of conversation, friendship and love, the female offers us these paltry substitutes:

"Great Art" and "Culture": The female "artist" attempts to solve her dilemma of not being able to live, of not being female, by constructing a highly artificial world in which the female is heroized, that is, displays female traits, and the female is reduced to highly limited, insipid subordinate roles, that is, to being female.

The female "artistic" aim being, not to communicate (having nothing inside her, she has nothing to say), but to disguise her animalism, she resorts to symbolism and obscurity ("deep" stuff). The vast majority of people, particularly the "educated" ones, lacking faith in their own judgment, humble, respectful of authority ("Mother knows best" is translated into adult language as "Critic knows best", "Writer knows best", "Ph.D knows best"), are easily conned into believing that obscurity, evasiveness, incomprehensibility, indirectness, ambiguity and boredom are marks of depth and brilliance.

"Great Art" proves that women are superior to women, that women are women, being labeled "Great Art", almost all of which, as the anti-feminists are fond of reminding us, was created by women. We know that "Great Art" is great because female authorities have told us so, and we can't claim otherwise, as only those with exquisite sensitivities far superior to ours can perceive and appreciate the greatness, the proof of their superior sensitivity being that they appreciate the slop that they appreciate.

Appreciating is the sole diversion of the "cultivated"; passive and incompetent, lacking imagination and wit, they must try to make do with that; unable to create their own diversions, to create a little world of their own, to affect in the smallest way their environments, they must accept what's given; unable to create or relate, they spectate. Absorbing "culture" is a desperate, frantic attempt to groove in an ungroovy world, to escape the horror of a sterile, mindless existence. "Culture" provides a sop to the egos of the incompetent, a means of rationalizing passive spectating; they can pride themselves on their ability to appreciate the "finer" things, to see a jewel where there is only a turd (they want to be admired for admiring). Lacking faith in their ability to change anything, resigned to the status quo, they have to see beauty in turds because, so far as they can see, turds are all they'll ever have.

The veneration of "Art" and "Culture"--besides leading many women into boring, passive activity that distracts from more important and rewarding activities, from cultivating active abilities--allows the "artist" to be set up as one possessing superior feelings, perceptions, insights and judgments, thereby undermining the faith of insecure women in the value and validity of their own feelings, perceptions, insights and judgments.

The female, having a very limited range of feelings and, consequently, very limited perceptions, insights and judgments, needs the "artist" to guide her, to tell her what life is all about. But the female "artist", being totally sexual, unable to relate to anything beyond her own physical sensations, having nothing to express beyond the insight that for the female life is meaningless and absurd, cannot be an artist. How can she who is not capable of life tell us what life is all about? A "male artist" is a contradiction in terms. A degenerate can only produce degenerate "art". The true artist is every self-confident, healthy female, and in a female society the only Art, the only Culture, will be conceited, kookie, funky females grooving on each other and on everything else in the universe.

Sexuality: Sex is not part of a relationship; on the contrary, it is a solitary experience, non-creative, a gross waste of time. The female can easily--far more easily than she may think--condition away her sex drive, leaving her completely cool and cerebral and free to pursue truly worthy relationships and activities; but the female, who seems to dig women sexually and who seeks constantly to arouse them, stimulates the highly-sexed female to frenzies of lust, throwing her into a sex bag from which few women ever escape. The lecherous female excited the lustful female; she has to--when the female transcends her body, rises above animalism, the female, whose ego consists of her pussy, will disappear.

Sex is the refuge of the mindless. And the more mindless the woman, the more deeply embedded in the female "culture", in short, the nicer she is, the more sexual she is. The nicest women in our "society" are raving sex maniacs. But, being just awfully, awfully nice they don't, of course, descend to fucking--that's uncouth--rather they make love, commune by means of their bodies and establish sensual rapport; the literary ones are attuned to the throb of Eros and attain a clutch upon the Universe; the religious have spiritual communion with the Divine Sensualism; the mystics merge with the Erotic Principle and blend with the Cosmos, and the acid heads contact their erotic cells.

On the other hand, those females least embedded in the female "Culture", the least nice, those crass and simple souls who reduce fucking to fucking, who are too childish for the grown-up world of suburbs, mortgages, mops and baby shit, too selfish to raise kids and husbands, too uncivilized to give a shit for anyone's opinion of them, too arrogant to respect Mother, the "Greats" or the deep wisdom of the Ancients, who trust only their own animal, gutter instincts, who

equate Culture with chicks, whose sole diversion is prowling for
emotional thrills and excitement, who are given to disgusting, nasty,
upsetting "scenes", hateful, violent bitches given to slamming those
who unduly irritate them in the teeth, who'd sink a shiv into a
woman's chest or ram an icepick up her asshole as soon as look at
her, if they knew they could get away with it, in short, those who, by
the standards of our "culture" are SCUW...these females are cool and
relatively cerebral and skirting asexuality.

Unhampered by propriety, niceness, discretion, public opinion,
"morals", the "respect" of assholes, always funky, dirty, low-down
SCUW gets around...and around and around...they've seen the whole
show--every bit of it-the fucking scene, the sucking scene, the dyke
scene--they've covered the whole waterfront, been under every dock
and pier--the peter pier, the pussy pier...you've got to go through a lot
of sex to get to anti-sex, and SCUW's been through it all, and they're
now ready for a new show; they want to crawl out from under the
dock, move, take off, sink out. But SCUW doesn't yet prevail;
SCUW's still in the gutter of our "society", which, if it's not deflected
from its present course and if the Bomb doesn't drop on it, will
hump itself to death.

Boredom: Life in a "society" made by and for creatures who, when
they are not grim and depressing are utter bores, can only be, when
not grim and depressing, an utter bore.

**Secrecy, Censorship, Suppression of Knowledge and Ideas, and
Exposes:** Every female's deep-seated, secret, most hideous fear is the
fear of being discovered to be not a female, but a female, a
subhuman animal. Although niceness, politeness and "dignity" suffice
to prevent her exposure on a personal level, in order to prevent the
general exposure of the female sex as a whole and to maintain her
unnatural dominant position in "society", the female must resort to:

1. Censorship. Responding reflexively to isolated words and phrases
rather than cerebrally to overall meanings, the female attempts to
prevent the arousal and discovery of her animalism by censoring not
only "pornography", but any work containing "dirty" words, no
matter in what context they are used.

2. Suppression of all ideas and knowledge that might expose her or
threaten her dominant position in "society". Much biological and
psychological data is suppressed, because it is proof of the female's

gross inferiority to the female. Also, the problem of womental illness will never be solved while the female maintains control, because first, women have a vested interest in it--only females who have very few of their marbles will allow females the slightest bit of control over anything, and second, the female cannot admit to the role that motherhood plays in causing womental illness.

3. Exposes. The female's chief delight in life--insofar as the dense, grim female can ever be said to delight in anything--is in exposing others. It doesn't much matter what they're exposed as, so long as they're exposed; it distracts attention from herself. Exposing others as enemy agents (Communists and Socialists) is one of her favorite pastimes, as it removes the source of the threat to her not only from herself, but from the country and the Western world. The bugs up her ass aren't in her; they're in Russia.

Distrust: Unable to empathize or feel affection or loyalty, being exclusively out for herself, the female has no sense of fair play; cowardly, needing constantly to pander to the female to win her approval, that she is helpless without, always on edge lest her animalism, her femaleness be discovered, always needing to cover up, she must lie constantly; being empty, she has no honor or integrity-- she doesn't know what those words mean. The female, in short, is treacherous, and the only appropriate attitude in a female "society" is cynicism and distrust.

Ugliness: Being totally sexual, incapable of cerebral or aesthetic responses, totally materialistic and greedy, the female, besides inflicting on the world "Great Art", has decorated her unlandscaped cities with ugly buildings (both inside and out), ugly decors, billboards, highways, cars, garbage trucks and, most notably, her own putrid self.

Hate and Violence: The female is eaten up with tension, with frustration at not being female, at not being capable of ever achieving satisfaction or pleasure of any kind; eaten up with hate--not rational hate that is directed against those who abuse or insult you--but irrational, indiscriminate hate...hatred, at bottom, of her own worthless self.

Violence serves as an outlet for her hate and, in addition--the female being capable only of sexual responses and needing very strong stimuli to stimulate her half-dead self--provides her with a little sexual thrill.

Disease and Death: All diseases are curable, and the aging process and death are due to disease; it is possible, therefore, never to age and to live forever. In fact, the problems of aging and death could be solved within a few years, if an all-out, massive scientific assault were made on the problem. This, however, will not occur within the female establishment, because:

1. The many female scientists who shy away from biological research, terrified of the discovery that females are females, and show marked preference for virile, "womanly" war and death programs.

2. The discouragement of many potential scientists from scientific careers by the rigidity, boringness, expensiveness, timeconsumingness and unfair exclusivity of our "higher" educational system.

3. Propaganda disseminated by insecure female professionals, who jealously guard their positions, so that only a highly select few can comprehend abstract scientific concepts.

4. Widespread lack of self-confidence brought about by the mother system that discourages many talented girls from becoming scientists.

5. Lack of automation. There now exists a wealth of data which, if sorted out and correlated, would reveal the cure for cancer and several other diseases and possibly the key to life itself. But the data is so massive it requires high speed computers to correlate it all. The institution of computers will be delayed interminably under the female control system, since the female has a horror of being replaced by machines.

6. The money system's insatiable need for new products. Most of the few scientists around who aren't working on death programs are tied up doing research for corporations.

7. The female likes death--it excites her sexually and, already dead inside, she wants to die.

Incapable of a positive state of happiness, which is the only thing that can justify one's existence, the female is, at best, relaxed, comfortable, neutral, and this condition is extremely short-lived, as boredom, a negative state, soon sets in; she is, therefore, doomed to an existence of suffering relieved only by occasional, fleeting stretches of restfulness, which state she can achieve only at the expense of some female. The female is, by her very nature, a leech, an emotional parasite and, therefore, not ethically entitled to live, as no one has the right to live at someone else's expense.

Just as humans have a prior right to existence over dogs by virtue of being more highly evolved and having a superior consciousness, so women have a prior right to existence over women. The elimination of any female is, therefore, a righteous and good act, an act highly beneficial to women as well as an act of mercy.

However, this moral issue will eventually be rendered academic by the fact that the female is gradually eliminating herself. In addition to engaging in the time-honored and classical wars and race riots, women are more and more either becoming lesbians or are obliterating themselves through drugs. The female, whether she likes it or not, will eventually take complete charge, if for no other reason than that she will have to--the female, for practical purposes, won't exist.

Accelerating this trend is the fact that more and more females are acquiring enlightened self-interest; they're realizing more and more that the female interest is **their** interest, that they can live only through the female and that the more the female is encouraged to live, to fulfill herself, to be a female and not a female, the more nearly she lives; she's coming to see that it's easier and more satisfactory to live **through** her than to try to **become** her and usurp her qualities, claim them as her own, push the female down and claim she's a female. The lesbian, who accepts her femaleness, that is, her passivity and total sexuality, her femininity, is also best served by women being truly female, as it would then be easier for her to be female, feminine. If women were wise they would seek to become really female, would do intensive biological research that would lead to women, by means of operations on the brain and nervous system, being able to be transformed in psyche, as well as body, into women.

Whether to continue to use females for reproduction or to reproduce in the laboratory will also become academic: what will happen when every female, twelve and over, is routinely taking the Pill and there are no longer any accidents? How many women will deliberately get or (if an accident) remain pregnant? No, Virginia, women don't just adore being brood mares, despite what the mass of robot, brainwashed women will say. When society consists of only the fully conscious the answer will be none. Should a certain percentage of women be set aside by force to serve as brood mares for the species? Obviously this will not do. The answer is laboratory reproduction of babies.

As for the issue of whether or not to continue to reproduce females, it doesn't follow that because the female, like disease, has always existed among us that she should continue to exist. When genetic control is possible--and it soon will be--it goes without saying that we should produce only whole, complete beings, not physical defects or deficiencies, including emotional deficiencies, such as femaleness. Just as the deliberate production of blind people would be highly immoral, so would be the deliberate production of emotional cripples.

Why produce even females? Why should there be future generations? What is their purpose? When aging and death are eliminated, why continue to reproduce? Why should we care what happens when we're dead? Why should we care that there is no younger generation to succeed us?

Eventually the natural course of events, of social evolution, will lead to total female control of the world and, subsequently, to the cessation of the production of females and, ultimately, to the cessation of the production of females.

But SCUW is impatient; SCUW is not consoled by the thought that future generations will thrive; SCUW wants to grab some thrilling living for itself. And, if a large majority of women were SCUW, they could acquire complete control of this country within a few weeks simply by withdrawing from the labor force, thereby paralyzing the entire nation. Additional measures, any one of which would be sufficient to completely disrupt the economy and everything else, would be for women to declare themselves off the money system, stop buying, just loot and simply refuse to obey all laws they don't care to obey. The police force, National Guard, Army, Navy and Marines combined couldn't squelch a rebellion of over half the population, particularly when it's made up of people they are utterly helpless without.

If all women simply left women, refused to have anything to do with any of them--ever, all women, the government, and the national economy would collapse completely. Even without leaving women, women who are aware of the extent of their superiority to and power over women, could acquire complete control over everything within a few weeks, could effect a total submission of females to females. In a sane society the female would trot along obediently after the female. The female is docile and easily led, easily subjected to the domination of any female who cares to dominate her. The female, in fact, wants desperately to be led by females, wants Mama in charge, wants to abandon herself to her care. But this is not a sane society, and most women are not even dimly aware of where they're at in relation to women.

The conflict, therefore, is not between females and females, but between SCUW--dominant, secure, self-confident, nasty, violent, selfish, independent, proud, thrill-seeking, free-wheeling, arrogant females, who consider themselves fit to rule the universe, who have free-wheeled to the limits of this "society" and are ready to wheel on to something far beyond what it has to offer--and nice, passive, accepting, "cultivated", polite, dignified, subdued, dependent, scared, mindless, insecure, approval-seeking Mother's Girls, who can't cope with the unknown, who want to continue to wallow in the sewer that is, at least, familiar, who want to hang back with the apes, who feel secure only with Big Mother standing by, with a big, strong woman to lean on and with a fat, hairy face in the White House, who are too cowardly to face up to the hideous reality of what a woman is, what Mother is, who have cast their lot with the swine, who have adapted themselves to animalism, feel superficially comfortable with it and know no other way of "life", who have reduced their minds, thoughts and sights to the female level, who, lacking sense, imagination and wit can have value only in a female "society", who can have a place in the sun, or, rather, in the slime, only as soothers, ego boosters, relaxers and breeders, who are dismissed as inconsequents by other females, who project their deficiencies, their femaleness, onto all females and see the female as a worm.

But SCUW is too impatient to hope and wait for the de-brainwashing of millions of assholes. Why should the swinging females continue to plod dismally along with the dull female ones? Why should the fates of the groovy and the creepy be intertwined? Why should the active and imaginative consult the passive and dull on social policy? Why should the independent be confined to the sewer along with the dependent who need Mother to cling to?

A small handful of SCUW can take over the country within a year by systematically fucking up the system, selectively destroying property, and murder:

SCUW will become members of the unwork force, the fuck-up force; they will get jobs of various kinds and unwork. For example, SCUW salesgirls will not charge for merchandise; SCUW telephone operators will not charge for calls; SCUW office and factory workers, in addition to fucking up their work, will secretly destroy equipment. SCUW will unwork at a job until fired, then get a new job to unwork at.

SCUW will forcibly relieve bus drivers, cab drivers and subway token sellers of their jobs and run buses and cabs and dispense free tokens to the public.

SCUW will destroy all useless and harmful objects--cars, store windows, "Great Art", etc.

Eventually SCUW will take over the airwaves--radio and TV networks--by forcibly relieving of their jobs all radio and TV employees who would impede SCUW's entry into the broadcasting studios.

SCUW will couple-bust--barge into mixed (female-female) couples, wherever they are, and bust them up.

SCUW will kill all women who are not in the Women Women's Auxiliary of SCUW.Women Women in the Women Women's Auxiliary are those women who are working diligently to eliminate themselves, women who, regardless of their motives, do good, women who are playing ball with SCUW. A few examples of the women in theWomen Women's Auxiliary are: women who kill women; biological scientists who are working on constructive programs, as opposed to biological warfare; journalists, writers, editors, publishers and producers who disseminate and promote ideas that will lead to the achievement of SCUW's goals; lesbians who, by their shimmering, flaming example, encourage other women to de-woman themselves and thereby make themselves relatively inoffensive; women who consistently give things away--money, things, services; women who tell it like it is (so far not one ever has), who put women straight, who reveal the truth about themselves, who give the mindless female females correct sentences to parrot, who tell them a woman's primary goal in life should be to squash the female sex (to aid women in this endeavor SCUW will conduct Turd Sessions, at which every female present will give a speech beginning with the sentence: "I am a turd, a lowly, abject turd," then proceed to list all the ways in which she is. Her reward for so doing will be the opportunity to sororitize after the session for a whole, solid hour with the SCUW who will be present. Nice, clean-living female women will be invited to the sessions to help clarify any doubts and misunderstandings they may have about the female sex); makers and promoters of sex books and movies, etc., who are hastening the day when all that will be shown on the screen will be Suck and Fuck (females, like the rats following the Pied Piper, will be lured by Pussy to their doom, will be overcome and submerged by and will eventually drown in the passive flesh that they are); drug pushers and advocates, who are hastening the dropping out of women.

Being in theWomen Women's Auxiliary is a necessary but not a sufficient condition for making SCUW's escape list; it's not enough to do good; to save their worthless asses women must also avoid evil. A few examples of the most obnoxious or harmful types are: rapists, politicians and all who are in their service (campaigners, members of political parties, etc.); lousy singers and musicians; Chairwomen of Boards; Breadwinners; landladies; owners of greasy spoons and restaurants that play Musak; "Great Artists"; cheap pikers and welchers; cops; tycoons; scientists working on death and destruction programs or for private industry (practically all scientists); liars and phonies; disc jockeys; women who intrude themselves in the slightest way on any strange female; real estate women; stock brokers; women who speak when they have nothing to say; women who loiter idly on the street and mar the landscape with their presence; double dealers; flim-flam artists; litterbugs; plagiarizers; women who in the slightest way harm any female; all women in the advertising industry; psychiatrists and clinical psychologists; dishonest writers, journalists, editors, publishers, etc.; censors on both the public and private levels; all members of the armed forces, including draftees (LBJ and McNamara give orders, but servicewomen carry them out) and particularly pilots (if the bomb drops, LBJ won't drop it; a pilot will). In the case of a woman whose behavior falls into both the good and bad categories, an overall subjective evaluation of her will be made to determine if her behavior is, in the balance, good or bad.

It is most tempting to pick off the female "Great Artists", double dealers, etc. along with the women, but that would be impractical, as there would be no one left; all women have a fink streak in them, to a great or lesser degree, but it stems from a lifetime of living among women. Eliminate women and women will shape up. Women are improvable; women are not, although their behavior is. When SCUW gets hot on their asses it'll shape up fast.

Simultaneously with the fucking-up, looting, couple-busting, destroying and killing, SCUW will recruit. SCUW, then, will consist of recruiters; the elite corps--the hard core activists (the fuck-ups, looters and destroyers) and the elite of the elite--the killers. Dropping out is not the answer; fucking-up is. Most women are already dropped out; they were never in. Dropping out gives control to those few who don't drop out; dropping out is exactly what the establishment leaders want; it plays into the hands of the enemy; it strengthens the system instead of undermining it, since it is based entirely on the non-participation, passivity, apathy and noninvolvement of the mass of women. Dropping out, however, is an excellent policy for women and SCUW will enthusiastically encourage it.

Looking inside yourself for salvation, contemplating your navel, is not, as the Drop Out people would have you believe, the answer. Happiness lies outside yourself, is achieved through interacting with others. Self-forgetfulness should be one's goal, not self-absorption. The female, capable of only the latter, makes a virtue of an irremediable fault and sets up self-absorption, not only as a good but as a Philosophical Good, and thus gets credit for being deep. SCUW will not picket, demonstrate, march or strike to attempt to achieve its ends. Such tactics are for nice, genteel ladies who scrupulously take only such action as is guaranteed to be ineffective. In addition, only decent, clean-living, female women, highly trained in submerging themselves in the species, act on a mob basis. SCUW consists of individuals; SCUW is not a mob, a blob. Only as many SCUW will do a job as are needed for the job. Also, SCUW, being cool and selfish, will not subject itself to getting rapped on the head with billy clubs; that's for the nice, "privileged, educated", middleclass ladies with a high regard for the touching faith in the essential goodness of Mother and policewomen. If SCUW ever marches, it will be over the President's stupid, sickening face; if SCUW ever strikes, it will be in the dark with a six-inch blade.

SCUW will always operate on a criminal as opposed to a civil disobedience basis, that is, as opposed to openly violating the law and going to jail in order to draw attention to an injustice. Such tactics acknowledge the rightness of the overall system and are used only to modify it slightly, change specific laws. SCUW is against the entire system, the very idea of law and government. SCUW is out to destroy the system, not attain certain rights within it. Also, SCUW--always selfish, always cool--will always aim to avoid detection and punishment. SCUW will always be furtive, sneaky, underhanded (although SCUW murders will always be known to be such).

Both destruction and killing will be selective and discriminate. SCUW is against half-crazed, indiscriminate riots, with no clear objective in mind, and in which many of your own kind are picked off. SCUW will never instigate, encourage or participate in riots of any kind or any other form of indiscriminate destruction. SCUW will coolly, furtively, stalk its prey and quietly move in for the kill. Destruction will never be such as to block off routes needed for the transportation of food and other essential supplies, contaminate or cut off the water supply, block streets and traffic to the extent that ambulances can't get through or impede the functioning of hospitals. SCUW will keep on destroying, looting, fucking-up and killing until the money-work system no longer exists and automation is completely instituted or until enough women co-operate with SCUW to make violence unnecessary to achieve these goals, that is, until enough women either unwork or quit work, start looting, leave women and refuse to obey all laws inappropriate to a truly civilized society. Many women will fall into line, but many others, who surrendered long ago to the enemy, who are so adapted to animalism, to femaleness, that they like restrictions and restraints, don't know what to do with freedom, will continue to be toadies and doormats, just as peasants in rice paddies remain peasants in rice paddies as one regime topples another. A few of the more volatile will whimper and sulk and throw their toys and dishrags on the floor, but SCUW will continue to steamroller over them.

A completely automated society can be accomplished very simply and quickly once there is a public demand for it. The blueprints for it are already in existence, and its construction will only take a few weeks with millions of people working at it. Even though off the money system, everyone will be most happy to pitch in and get the automated society built; it will mark the beginning of a fantastic new era, and there will be a celebration atmosphere accompanying the construction.

The elimination of money and the complete institution of automation are basic to all other SCUW reforms; without these two the others can't take place; with them the others will take place very rapidly. The government will automatically collapse. With complete automation it will be possible for every woman to vote directly on every issue by means of an electronic voting machine in her house. Since the government is occupied almost entirely with regulating economic affairs and legislating against purely private matters, the elimination of money and with it the elimination of females who wish to legislate "morality" will mean that there will be practically no issues to vote on.

After the elimination of money there will be no further need to kill women; they will be stripped of the only power they have over psychologically independent females. They will be able to impose themselves only on the doormats, who like to be imposed on. The rest of the women will be busy solving the few remaining unsolved problems before planning their agenda for eternity and Utopia-- completely revamping educational programs so that millions of women can be trained within a few months for high level intellectual work that now requires years of training (this can be done very easily once our educational goal is to educate and not to perpetuate an academic and intellectual elite); solving the problems of disease and old age and death and completely redesigning our cities and living quarters. Many women will for a while continue to think they dig women, but as they become accustomed to female society and as they become absorbed in their projects, they will eventually come to see the utter uselessness and banality of the female.

The few remaining women can exist out their puny days dropped out on drugs or strutting around in drag or passively watching the highpowered female in action, fulfilling themselves as spectators, vicarious livers (*It will be electronically possible for her to tune in to any specific female she wants to and follow in detail her every movement. The females will kindly, obligingly consent to this, as it won't hurt them in the slightest and it is a marvelously kind and humane way to treat their unfortunate, handicapped fellow beings.*) or breeding in the cow pasture with the toadies, or they can go off to the nearest friendly suicide center where they will be quietly, quickly and painlessly gassed to death.

Prior to the institution of automation, to the replacement of females by machines, the female should be of use to the female, wait on her, cater to her slightest whim, obey her every command, be totally subservient to her, exist in perfect obedience to her will, as opposed to the completely warped, degenerate situation we have now of women, not only not existing at all, cluttering up the world with their ignominious presence, but being pandered to and groveled before by the mass of females, millions of women piously worshipping before the Golden Calf, the dog leading the master on the leash, when in fact the female, short of being a drag queen, is least miserable when abjectly prostrate before the female, a complete slave. Rational women want to be squashed, stepped on, crushed and crunched, treated as the curs, the filth that they are, have their repulsiveness confirmed.

The sick, irrational women, those who attempt to defend themselves against their disgustingness, when they see SCUW barreling down on them, will cling in terror to Big Mama with her Big Bouncy Boobies, but Boobies won't protect them against SCUW; Big Mama will be clinging to Big Mother, who will be in the corner shitting in her forceful, dynamic pants. Women Women who are rational, however, won't kick or struggle or raise a distressing fuss, but will just sit back, relax, enjoy the show and ride the waves to their demise.